How did the universe begin? How hot is the sun? How long does it take to get to the moon? What would it feel like to travel in space?

Explore the answers to these questions and more in . . .

Magic Tree House® Research Guide
SPACE

A nonfiction companion to
Midnight on the Moon

It's Jack and Annie's very own guide to the secrets of the universe!

Including:
- Stars
- Planets
- Space travel
- Life on other planets

And much more!

Here's what people are saying
about the Magic Tree House®
Research Guides:

I like these books so much when my mom reads them to me that I can hardly wait to be able to read them all by myself.
—J.D.M., age 6

I like them because they have cool information and are fun to read!—Ryan W., age 8

We loved reading the Research Guides as a family. We all learned from them. Thanks!—Joy H., parent

Yes! Finally, comprehensive guides that will be able to serve as a handbook for the entire research process from beginning to end!—Cheryl R., third-grade teacher

The Magic Tree House Research Guides and the Magic Tree House stories go hand in hand to encourage kids to read for fun and read to learn!—Sandra G., media specialist

Magic Tree House® Research Guide
SPACE

A nonfiction companion to
Midnight on the Moon

by Will Osborne
and Mary Pope Osborne

illustrated by Sal Murdocca

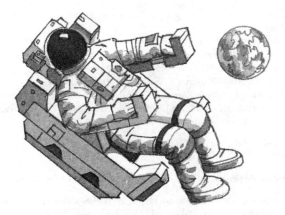

A STEPPING STONE BOOK™
Random House 🏠 New York

www.randomhouse.com/magictreehouse

Library of Congress Cataloging-in-Publication Data
Osborne, Will.
Space / by Will Osborne and Mary Pope Osborne ;
illustrated by Sal Murdocca. p. cm. — (Magic tree house research guide)
"A nonfiction companion to Midnight on the Moon."
ISBN 0-375-81356-X (trade) — ISBN 0-375-91356-4 (lib. bdg.)
1. Astronomy—Juvenile literature. 2. Space flight—Juvenile literature.
[1. Astronomy. 2. Space flight.] I. Osborne, Mary Pope. II. Murdocca, Sal, ill.
III. Title. IV. Series. QB46. O76 2002 520—dc21 2001048202

Printed in the United States of America First Edition February 2002
20 19 18

Random House, Inc. New York, Toronto, London, Sydney, Auckland

RANDOM HOUSE and colophon are registered trademarks and A STEPPING STONE
BOOK and colophon are trademarks of Random House, Inc. MAGIC TREE HOUSE
is a registered trademark of Mary Pope Osborne; used under license.

For Wil and Melanie Aiken

Scientific Consultant:

STEPHANIE L. PARELLO, Astronomy Education Coordinator, Hayden Planetarium, New York City.

Education Consultant:

MELINDA MURPHY, Media Specialist, Reed Elementary School, Cypress Fairbanks Independent School District, Houston, Texas.

Very special thanks to Dr. Alan J. Friedman, Ph.D., Director, New York Hall of Science, for his professional hospitality, meticulous marble mathematics, stunning photographic contribution, and unflagging moral support.

We would also like to thank Paul Coughlin for his ongoing photographic contribution to the series and, again, our wonderful, creative team at Random House: Joanne Yates, Helena Winston, Diane Landolf, Cathy Goldsmith, Mallory Loehr, and, of course, our wonderful editor, Shana Corey.

SPACE

Contents

1. Astronomy   13

2. The Universe   27

3. The Sun   35

4. Our Solar System   45

5. Space Travel   77

6. From Earth to the Moon   87

7. Space Travel Today   99

8. Living and Working in Space   111

9. The Future   121

Doing More Research   126

Index   133

Dear Readers,

We had a really exciting space adventure in <u>Midnight on the Moon</u>. When we got back to Frog Creek, we wanted to learn more about the moon and space travel, and about all the stars and planets. So we set out on another mission: <u>Research!</u>

We went to the library and checked out books about astronomy.

We watched a video about the first men to walk on the moon.

We found a CD-ROM that helped us learn more about planets and stars.

Finally, we went to a science museum and saw a great show about the birth of the universe 15 billion years ago!

Now we want to share our research with you.

So get your notebook, get your backpack, and get ready to blast off on your own research mission in <u>Space</u>!

Jack

Annie

1

Astronomy

People have always been interested in space.

Cave people painted pictures of the night sky on the walls of their caves. Ancient Egyptians believed there were sun gods and moon goddesses. The ancient Chinese built stone towers so they could study the sky more closely.

Over the centuries, people began to write down what they learned from looking at the skies. They gave the planets names. They made maps of the stars. They noted changes in the sky from month to month and from year to year.

Ancient Aztec calendar

The first calendars were based on changes people saw in the heavens.

The study of the skies became the very first science. This science is called *astronomy* (uh-STRAHN-uh-mee).

Ancient Greek Astronomy

Nearly 2,000 years ago, a Greek

14

astronomer named Ptolemy (TAHL-uh-mee) wrote the first books about astronomy. In his books, Ptolemy described how he thought the stars and planets moved in the sky.

Ptolemy (A.D. 90–165)

Ptolemy believed that Earth was at the center of everything. He thought the sun, stars, and everything else in the sky traveled around Earth.

For over a thousand years, nearly everyone accepted Ptolemy's ideas as facts. They did not know that Ptolemy's "facts" were completely wrong.

Copernicus

Nicolaus Copernicus (nihk-uh-LAY-us koh-PUR-nuh-kus) was a Polish astronomer. He lived nearly 1,400 years after Ptolemy.

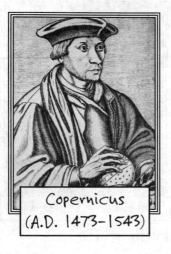

Copernicus
(A.D. 1473-1543)

Copernicus studied Ptolemy's ideas for a long time. He knew something was not right.

Copernicus figured out that the sun does *not* travel around Earth. It's really the other way around! Earth and all the other planets travel around the sun.

Copernicus was afraid people would not accept his ideas. So he waited until he was about to die to let the world know what he thought. In 1543, he published a book that said Ptolemy was wrong.

Copernicus's fears came true. People were furious when they read his book! They liked thinking that Earth was the center of everything.

For many years, it was against the law even to *talk* about Copernicus's

Oh, wow! Copernicus died just a few months after his book was published.

ideas. The few people who believed Copernicus kept their belief secret.

Galileo

One person who believed Copernicus was an Italian astronomer named Galileo Galilei (gal-uh-LAY-oh gal-uh-LAY). Galileo was sure Copernicus was right. But he didn't know how to prove it.

Galileo (1564–1642)

One day, Galileo heard about a new invention. The invention was what we now call a *telescope*. The telescope made distant things seem closer.

Galileo couldn't believe that no one had used a telescope to study the sky! He was so excited by this idea that he built a telescope of his own.

The first telescopes were used mostly on battlefields.

17

Galileo's telescope

When Galileo peered through his telescope into the night sky, modern astronomy was born.

Galileo saw rings around the planet Saturn.

Saturn

He saw moons circling the planet Jupiter.

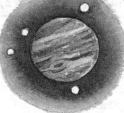

Jupiter

He saw that the planet Venus seemed to change shape, just like our moon.

And he saw that there were millions and millions of stars—far more than anyone had ever imagined.

Venus

The longer Galileo looked into the heavens, the more certain he became that Earth was *not* the center of everything!

Galileo studied the sky for the next 30 years. He wrote many books about his discoveries. Near the end of his life, he was arrested for teaching his ideas to others. He died trying to show people that Copernicus was right.

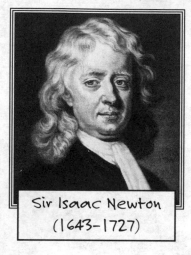

Sir Isaac Newton
(1643-1727)

Sir Isaac Newton

Isaac Newton was an English scientist. He made many discoveries. His most important discovery was the *law of gravity*.

Gravity is the invisible force that pulls everything on Earth toward the ground. Without gravity, we'd all float away!

Newton thought it was gravity that kept the moon traveling around Earth. He thought the sun might have gravity, too. That would explain why Earth and the other planets kept traveling around the sun instead of flying off into space.

Newton's ideas about gravity helped people understand and accept the theories of Copernicus and Galileo.

Theories are ideas that haven't been proven by science.

20

Early Astronomers

Ptolemy

Copernicus

Galileo

Newton

The Big Mistake

Copernicus, Galileo, and Newton were on the right path to understanding space. But they made one big mistake. They all thought that *everything* in space traveled around the sun.

Over time, astronomers have learned much more. They've learned that far from being the center of everything, the sun is just another star among billions and billions of stars. And they've learned that Earth is a tiny speck in a universe so big it's almost impossible to imagine.

Jack and Annie Present: Telescopes—Then and Now

Hans Lippershey (HAHNS LIP-ur-shay) invented the telescope in 1608. Lippershey was a Dutch eyeglass maker. Stories say he got the idea by watching his children play with lenses for his eyeglasses.

Sir Isaac Newton invented a telescope that used mirrors to see much farther into space.

Newton's telescope

Telescopes that use mirrors are called <u>reflecting</u> telescopes.

The *Hubble Space Telescope* is a telescope that travels in space. It sends pictures of planets and stars back to computers on Earth. The Hubble can see objects that are billions and billions of miles away.

 The Hubble Space Telescope was launched in 1990.

The biggest telescope in the world is called the *Very Large Telescope*. The Very Large Telescope is really several telescopes linked by computers. The people

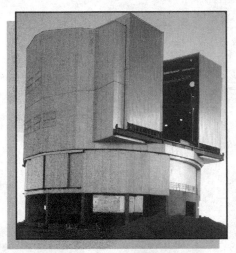

building the Very Large Telescope say that when it is complete, it could be powerful enough to see a person waving to Earth from the moon!

The Very Large Telescope is still being built in Chile.

Hello, Jack!

2

The Universe

The *universe* is everything there is. It is the sun and Earth and all the other planets and stars and all the space between them. It is full of dust and rocks and ice and gas. Mostly it is full of nothing—just trillions and trillions of miles of empty space.

The Birth of the Universe
The universe was born so long ago that no one knows for sure how it happened.

Today, most astronomers think the universe began with a huge explosion. They call the explosion the *Big Bang*. They think that it happened about 15 billion years ago.

Two things happened at the moment of the Big Bang. First, the stuff that would

Millions, Billions, and Trillions

The universe is *huge*. We have to use very big numbers when we talk about distances in the universe and the number of stars in the universe.

How much is a <u>million</u>?

A million marbles would fill the inside of a small car!

become everything in the universe came into being. Second, the universe began *expanding*. That means it went flying in all directions, moving farther and farther away from the spot where the Big Bang happened.

The universe is still expanding today!

How much is a <u>billion</u>?

A billion marbles would fill the inside of a two-story house!

How much is a <u>trillion</u>?

A trillion marbles would fill the biggest domed stadium right up to the roof!

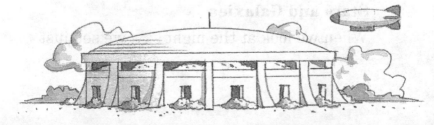

The universe expanded *very* quickly after the Big Bang. At the moment of the explosion, the whole universe was smaller than the head of a pin. Within a second, it was billions of times bigger than Earth.

For billions of years after the Big Bang, everything in the universe was just very, very hot gas. As the universe expanded and cooled, some of the gas began to clump together. The clumps grew into huge, fiery balls. These balls of hot gas became the first stars.

Birth of the Universe

Big Bang

Universe gets bigger and bigger

Gas balls form

Gas balls become stars

Stars and Galaxies

When we look at the night sky, we see just

a few of the stars that are in the universe. Even on the clearest night, only about 2,000 stars can be seen without a telescope. Astronomers think there may be as many as *10 billion trillion* stars in the universe!

Stars we can see = 2,000
Stars in the universe =
10,000,000,000,000,000,000,000

Stars are grouped together in *galaxies*. Most galaxies contain hundreds of billions of stars.

All the stars we can see are part of a galaxy called the *Milky Way*. There are more than 200 billion stars in the Milky Way. One of those stars is our sun.

Some stars are smaller than Earth. Others are 300 times larger than the sun!

Light-years

Astronomers measure distances in space in *light-years*. A light-year is the distance light can travel through space in one year. One light-year = 5,880 billion miles.

The sun is the star closest to Earth. It takes light from the sun about eight minutes to reach Earth. The next closest star is Proxima Centauri (PRAHK-suh-muh sen-TAW-ree). It takes light from Proxima Centauri about *four years* to

Proxima Centauri

Light—Spends four years traveling through space

Earth

reach Earth! So astronomers say that Proxima Centauri is *four light-years* away.

It takes light from distant stars billions of years to reach Earth. By the time it gets here, the stars are billions of years older than they were when the light left them. So we really see the stars as they used to be! Looking at the stars is like looking into the past.

3

The Sun

The sun is a star like all the other stars in the sky. It looks bigger and brighter than other stars because it is much closer to Earth.

The sun is 93 million miles from Earth. The next closest star is more than 20 *trillion* miles away!

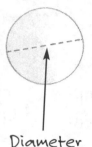

Diameter

The sun is a medium-sized star. It's about 865,000 miles in diameter. Compared to Earth, it's gigantic! Over a million Earths could fit inside the sun.

Heat and Light

The center of the sun is called the *core*. The sun's core is like a giant fiery furnace. But the fire of the sun is not an ordinary fire. No ordinary fire could warm Earth from 93 million miles away!

The fire at the center of the sun is called a *nuclear reaction* (NOO-klee-ur re-AK-shun). It is like millions of bombs exploding every second. These explosions produce lots and lots of energy.

The energy travels from the sun's core to the surface. When it reaches the surface, it shoots into space as heat and light.

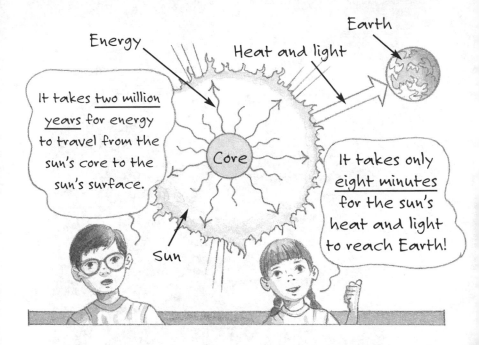

Spots, Flares, and Prominences

Since the sun is a ball of gas, its surface is not solid like Earth's. It is always changing, like the surface of a pot of boiling water.

There are often dark patches on the surface of the sun. These dark patches are called *sunspots*. Sunspots look dark because they are not quite as hot as the rest of the sun's surface. Most sunspots are many times bigger than Earth.

sunspot

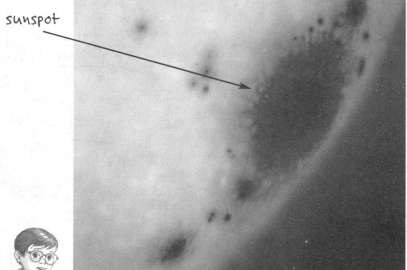

Giant bursts of light and heat sometimes explode above sunspots. These are called *solar flares*. Solar flares are twice as hot as the surface of the sun. They are also much brighter.

Prominences   (PRAH-muh-nens-iz)

are loops of fiery gas that leap out into space, then back to the sun's surface. Prominences can last for many hours.

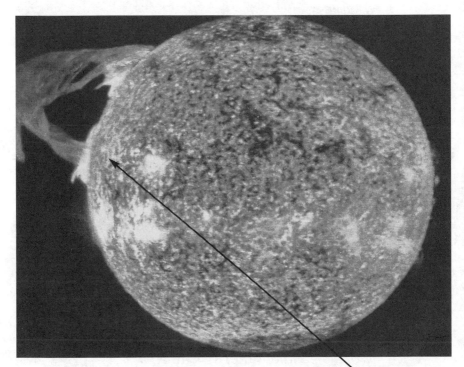

Most prominences are so big they could wrap around Earth more than ten times!

The Life of the Sun

The sun is what astronomers call a *yellow dwarf* star.

As it grows older, the sun will get bigger and cooler. It will also change color. It will become a *red giant*.

It will then get smaller and smaller until it shrinks to about the size of Earth. It will then be a *white dwarf*.

After it becomes a white dwarf, the sun will lose all its heat and light. But don't worry—astronomers think this won't happen for another 5 billion years!

Red giant

White dwarf

Importance of the Sun

The sun creates our weather. Without the sun, there would be no wind, no clouds, no rain.

Without the sun, there would be no plants or animals. There would be no life on Earth at all.

Without the sun, Earth would be just a cold, dark chunk of rock in space.

The sun is one of trillions of stars. But it is *our* star. It is the center of our tiny part of the universe.

Eclipses

Sometimes as the moon travels around Earth, it blocks the light from the sun. When this happens, we have a *solar eclipse* (SOH-lur ee-KLIPS).

The word solar comes from Sol, the ancient Roman god of the sun.

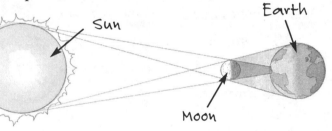

Sun

Earth

Moon

If the moon blocks the sun completely, we have a *total solar eclipse*.

WARNING!
Never look directly at the sun, even during an eclipse. It can harm your eyes. Don't do it!

42

Many ancient people were frightened by eclipses. The ancient Chinese thought a solar eclipse meant a dragon was eating the sun!

Total solar eclipse, February 16, 1980, Konarak, India.

Some of the planets are farther apart than they seem in this picture. The differences in their sizes have also been changed. The artist did this so everything would fit.

4

Our Solar System

Our part of space is called our *solar system*. Our solar system is the sun and everything that travels around it.

Birth of the Solar System

Like all stars, the sun was born in a cloud of dust and gas. Most astronomers think everything else in our solar system came from the same cloud.

As the cloud swirled around the

newborn sun, dust particles bumped into each other. They stuck together and formed clumps. The clumps grew bigger and bigger. Eventually they became planets, moons, asteroids, comets, and meteoroids. These are the members of our solar system.

Our Solar System

Sun

Planets

Moons

Asteroids

Comets

Meteoroids

All the members of our solar system travel around the sun in paths called *orbits*. The sun's gravity holds the mem-

46

bers of our solar system in their orbits. It keeps them from flying off into space.

Planets

Planets are the largest members of our solar system besides the sun. Some planets are rocky and solid like Earth. Others are big balls of gas.

Planets travel around the sun at different speeds. One trip around the sun is a planet's *year*.

Planets also *rotate* as they travel around the sun. One rotation is a planet's *day*.

Rotate means to spin like a top.

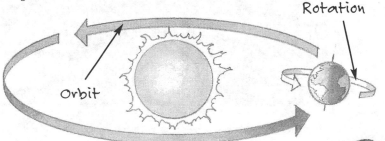

Rotation

Orbit

Even when we're sitting still, we're really traveling in at least two directions!

Moons

Many planets have *moons*. Moons are chunks of rock that travel with a planet in space. Moons orbit a planet as the planet orbits the sun. The gravity of a planet holds its moons in their orbits.

Jupiter and one of its moons.

Asteroids

Asteroids (AAS-tuh-roidz) are space rocks. They are much smaller than planets. The biggest are larger than an Earth mountain. The smallest are the size of pebbles.

If all the billions of asteroids in the asteroid belt were combined, they would still be smaller than our moon.

Asteroid Ida is a large asteroid that has its own moon.

A few asteroids orbit very close to the sun. But most travel in a big group between the planets Mars and Jupiter. This group of asteroids is called the *asteroid belt.*

49

Comets

Comets are balls of ice and space dust. Most comets orbit in very distant regions of space. Only a few ever travel close enough to Earth to be seen without telescopes.

The sun's heat causes passing comets to give off streams of gas and dust. These streams are called *tails*. Comet tails can be several million miles long.

Halley's comet, 1986

Many scientists think dinosaurs were wiped out by a huge comet or asteroid that hit Earth 65 million years ago.

Meteoroids

Meteoroids (MEE-tee-uh-roidz) are pieces of space rock or bits of space dust.

Earth bumps into millions of meteoroids as it orbits the sun. Most burn up when they enter Earth's atmosphere. The larger ones can be seen as streaks of light in the night sky. They are called *meteors*. When there are many meteors in the same part of the sky, it's called a *meteor shower*.

Earth's <u>atmosphere</u> is the invisible blanket of oxygen and other gases that surrounds it.

People sometimes call meteors <u>shooting stars</u> or <u>falling stars</u>, but they're not stars at all!

Some meteoroids fall to Earth without burning up completely. A meteoroid that lands on Earth is called a *meteorite*.

 This meteorite weighs 34 tons. It fell on Greenland 10,000 years ago.

A few meteorites are the size of boulders. But most are just tiny specks of dust. Several hundred tons of meteorite dust fall to Earth every day. So when you clean your room, you might be sweeping up a tiny bit of dust from outer space!

A <u>ton</u> is 2,000 pounds.

Turn the page to meet all the members of our solar system.

This way

Our Solar System

Mercury

Named after the Roman messenger god

Diameter: 3,030 miles

Temperature: -300° to 870°F

Mercury is the planet closest to the sun. It moves around the sun very quickly. A year on Mercury is less than three Earth months long!

Years may be short on Mercury, but days are l-o-n-g! That's because Mercury rotates very slowly as it moves around the sun. One day on Mercury (sunrise to sunrise) equals about 176 Earth days. That's nearly six months!

Mercury is a dry, rocky planet. It has craters like our moon.

Earth

Mercury

These pictures show each
planet's size compared to Earth's size.

Venus is the easiest planet to find in the sky. It looks like a big star that shines brightest just after sunset or just before dawn.

Earth   Venus

Venus

Named after the Roman goddess of love
  and beauty
Diameter: 7,520 miles
Temperature: averages 870°F

Venus is sometimes called Earth's twin sister. That's because Venus is almost the same size as Earth. It's also Earth's closest neighbor planet.

Venus is really very different from Earth. First of all, it's the hottest place in the solar system besides the sun. The temperature on Venus is more than four times hotter than boiling water!

Even if humans could stand the heat, they couldn't live on Venus. The air is poison! And it's so thick and heavy that a human being would be crushed before he or she even tried to breathe it!

Earth

Name comes from an Anglo-Saxon word
   meaning "land"
Diameter: 7,926 miles
Temperature: -129° to 136°F

From space, Earth looks like a beautiful blue and white marble. The white is from the clouds that swirl around our planet. The blue is from the water that covers two-thirds of Earth's surface.

Earth feels very solid to us. But below the surface, there is hot, melting rock and metal. The heat inside Earth sometimes causes volcanoes and earthquakes.

Many astronomers think Earth's water came from a storm of icy comets that hit Earth when it was forming.

59

The Moon

Also called Luna, after the twin sister of
   the Roman sun god

Diameter: 2,155 miles

Temperature: -300° to 260°F

The moon is about 240,000 miles from
Earth. The surface of the moon is gray and
rocky. There is no water, air, or wind.
There is a layer of dust over everything.
There is no atmosphere on the moon to
scatter the sunlight, so the sky is always
black.

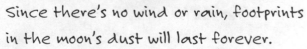

Since there's no wind or rain, footprints
in the moon's dust will last forever.

The moon's gravity is much weaker than Earth's. If you weigh 60 pounds on Earth, you would only weigh 10 pounds on the moon. That means you could jump really high!

We talk about the moon "shining." But the moon doesn't really shine at all. It just reflects light from the sun.

Moon   Earth

Mars is sometimes called the red planet. That's because the soil on Mars is full of red rust.

Earth

Mars

62

Mars

Named for the Roman god of war
Diameter: 4,218 miles
Temperature: -190° to 90°F

Mars is the planet that is most like Earth. Mars has mountains, deserts, and volcanoes. Its year has seasons like our year. A day on Mars is about the same length as a day on Earth.

Still, Mars is very different from Earth. There is almost no oxygen in the air, so humans couldn't breathe. There is no rain, so it is always dry and dusty. Dust in the thin air makes the Mars sky look pink instead of blue.

Mars also has two moons! The moons are tiny—the bigger one is only 16 miles across. And they're not round—they're shaped like potatoes!

Potato

Mars' moon

Jupiter

Named for the leader of all the Roman
  gods
Diameter: 88,846 miles
Temperature: averages -240°F

Jupiter is the biggest planet in the solar
system. It's twice as big as all the other
planets put together.

Jupiter is called a "gas giant" planet.
That's because there's no solid ground anywhere. It is a gigantic ball of gas with a hot
liquid center.

Jupiter is covered with white, blue, and
brown stripes. The stripes are really clouds
made of different gases. There is also a
giant red spot on Jupiter that's more than
twice as big as Earth. The spot is a storm
that has been raging for over 300 years.

Jupiter has
28 moons!

Earth   Jupiter

Saturn has more moons than any other planet. Astronomers think there are at least 30!

Saturn   Earth

Saturn

Named for Jupiter's father, the Roman
   god of the harvest

Diameter: 74,900 miles

Temperature: averages –300°F

Like Jupiter, Saturn is a gas giant. It moves *very* slowly around the sun. One year on Saturn equals 30 years on Earth!

Saturn is called the ringed planet. All the gas giant planets have rings, but Saturn's are much, much bigger.

Saturn's rings are made of pieces of ice and rock that orbit the planet. Some astronomers think they were made by comets crashing into some of Saturn's inner moons and smashing them to pieces.

Uranus

Named for Saturn's father, the Roman
   god of the sky
Diameter: 31,760 miles
Temperature: averages -350°F

Uranus is a cold planet. It is covered with green clouds. Beneath the clouds is a sea of water and gases.

Uranus has rings, too. Its rings are made of ice and rock like Saturn's. But they are much smaller.

The most unusual thing about Uranus is how it spins as it travels around the sun. Astronomers think Uranus might have been knocked sideways by a comet or asteroid billions of years ago. So instead of spinning like a top as it orbits, it rolls like a bowling ball. Because of Uranus's unusual spin, a night on Uranus can last for 42 Earth years!

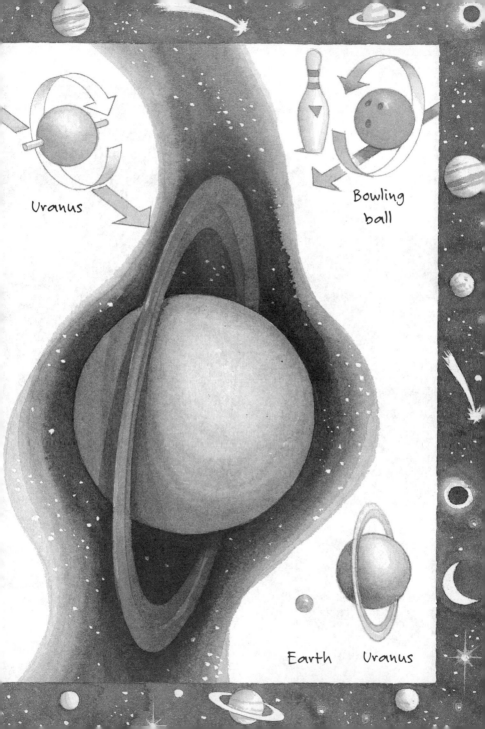

Uranus

Bowling ball

Earth   Uranus

Neptune   Earth

Neptune

Named for the Roman god of the sea

Diameter: 30,755 miles

Temperature: averages -370°F

Neptune is very similar to Uranus. It's about the same size. It's very cold. It has several rings.

There are some differences, though. Neptune looks blue instead of green. That's because its atmosphere is made of different kinds of gases. And Neptune has much wilder weather than Uranus. There are storms on Neptune with winds over 1,000 miles per hour. That's ten times faster than the winds in a hurricane on Earth.

Neptune has eight moons. One of Neptune's moons orbits backward! It's the only moon in the solar system that orbits in the opposite direction of its planet.

Pluto

Named for the Roman god of the
  underworld

Diameter: 1,485 miles

Temperature: averages -390°F

Pluto is so far from Earth that astronomers don't know very much about it. They do know that it is always dark and always cold. It's also tiny. It is smaller than Earth's moon.

Many astronomers today think Pluto shouldn't be called a planet at all! They think it's more like a large icy comet.

Pluto's moon, Charon, is almost as big as Pluto itself!

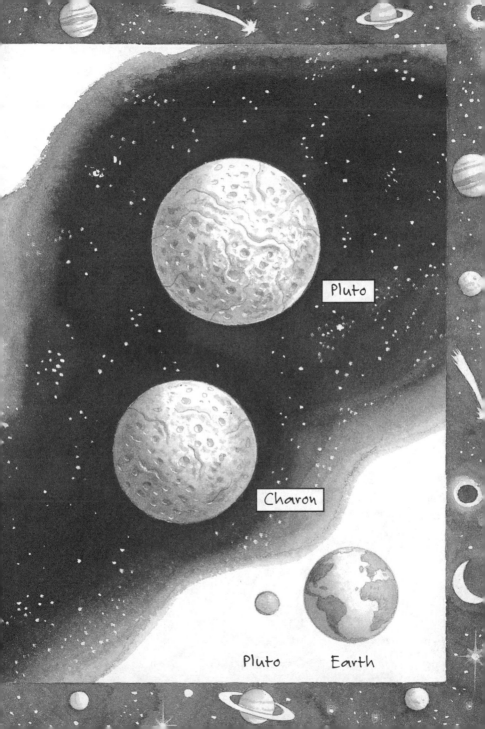

Pluto

Charon

Pluto   Earth

Jack and Annie Present: Name That Planet!

Here's a fun way to remember the order of the planets. The first letter of each word in this sentence is the first letter of one of the planets' names, moving from the sun out:

<u>M</u>y <u>V</u>ery <u>E</u>ager <u>M</u>other <u>J</u>ust <u>S</u>erved <u>U</u>s <u>N</u>ine <u>P</u>ickles.

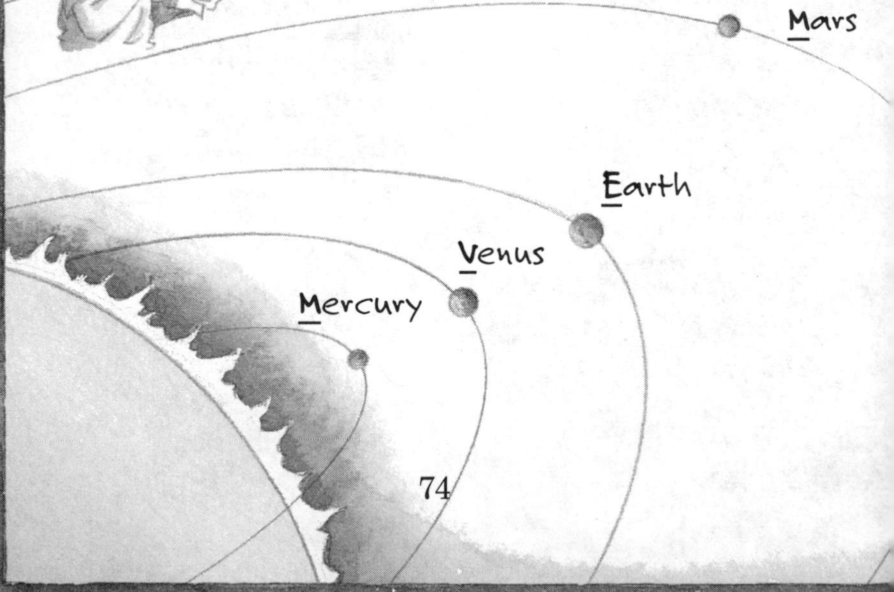

<u>M</u>ars

<u>E</u>arth

<u>V</u>enus

<u>M</u>ercury

Pluto

Neptune

Uranus

Saturn

Jupiter

75

5

Space Travel

When astronomers talk about *space* or *outer space*, they usually mean anything beyond Earth's atmosphere.

There is no line that marks where Earth's atmosphere ends and space begins. But most scientists agree that anything flying higher than 100 miles above Earth is traveling in space.

Spacecraft

A *spacecraft* is anything that travels in space carrying people or equipment. To get into space, a spacecraft has to escape Earth's gravity. The force of gravity is so strong that a spacecraft must travel 25,000 miles per hour to do that. That's 12 times faster than the fastest jet plane!

Engines like those in cars and jets are not powerful enough to send a spacecraft into space. Rockets are the only way so far.

Rockets were invented by the Chinese about 1,000 years ago. They were first used as weapons and fireworks.

Rockets

Rockets work by burning special fuel at very hot temperatures. When rocket fuel burns, the intense heat forces hot gas out of the bottom of the rocket. If the force is powerful enough, the hot gas pushes the

rocket off the ground, through the atmosphere, and into space.

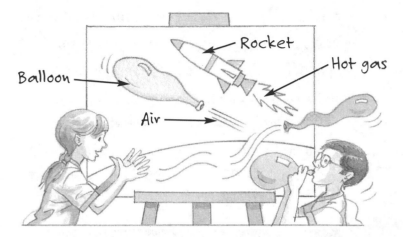

Rocket engines work sort of like
balloons.

If you let a balloon go without tying the
end, the air rushes out and pushes the balloon away from you.

In the same way, gases rushing out the
back end of a rocket push the rocket away
from Earth.

The Space Race

About 60 years ago, scientists in the Soviet Union and the United States began using rockets to try to put a spacecraft into space. The Soviets were the first to be successful.

On October 4, 1957, Soviet scientists launched the first man-made *satellite* into space. The satellite was called *Sputnik* (SPUT-nihk).

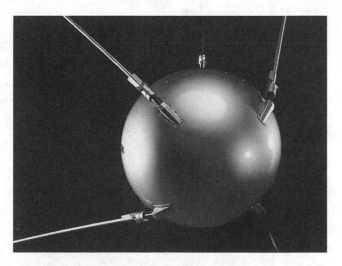

Sputnik was about the size of a beach ball.

Four months later, the United States put its own satellite into orbit. The "space race" between the United States and the Soviet Union had begun.

Astronauts and Cosmonauts

Over the next few years, the Soviet Union and the United States trained teams of people to get them ready for space travel. Members of the American team were called *astronauts*, which means "travelers to the stars." Members of the Soviet team were called *cosmonauts*, which means "travelers to the cosmos." *Cosmos* is another word for the universe.

The first U.S. satellite was called Explorer.

Finally, on April 12, 1961, a cosmonaut named Yuri Gagarin (YOO-ree guh-GAH-run) made one orbit of Earth in a

Soviet spacecraft. His flight lasted less than two hours. But Yuri Gagarin will be remembered forever as the first person to travel in space.

Yuri Gagarin

The President's Challenge

The president of the United States, John F. Kennedy, saw that the U.S. was losing the space race. So after Yuri Gagarin's flight, he made a bold promise. He said that the American space program would land a man on the moon before the end of the 1960s.

For the next eight years, nearly 400,000 Americans worked to make the president's words come true.

President Kennedy said we decided to go to the moon not because it was easy, but because it was hard.

The first flights into space were short but important. They proved that humans could travel in space and return safely to Earth.

Alan Shepard

Alan Shepard was the first American in space. On May 5, 1961, he took a 15-minute "hop" into space and splashed back into the ocean.

In 1962, John Glenn became the first American to orbit Earth. He returned to space 36 years later, at age 77.

John Glenn

Valentina Tereshkova

In 1963, Valentina Tereshkova, a cosmonaut, became the first woman to travel in space. She spent three days orbiting Earth.

Two Soviet dogs, Strelka and Belka, along with 40 mice and two rats, were the first animals to travel in space and return safely to Earth. They spent a day in space in 1960.

Strelka and Belka

85

6

From Earth to the Moon

Landing people on the moon was a much harder job than just getting a person into space.

A trip to the moon and back would take at least a week. When President Kennedy made his promise, no one had been in space longer than a few hours!

There were other problems as well. In 1961, there were no good pictures of the moon's surface. Astronauts would need "moon maps" to help them find a good landing spot. Also, no one had ever spent time in space outside a spacecraft. Astronauts on the moon would need special suits to protect them from the moon's very hot and cold temperatures.

American scientists and engineers worked very hard to solve all these problems.

A **probe** is an unmanned spacecraft controlled completely from Earth.

In 1961, they began sending *probes* to the moon. In 1964, one of the probes took very clear pictures of the moon's surface. The pictures helped scientists find a safe place for the astronauts to land.

In 1965, Ed White became the first American to "walk" in space. He spent 21 minutes outside a spacecraft as it orbited Earth. He wore a space suit that let him breathe and protected him from the cold.

Ed White said that going back inside the spacecraft after walking in space was the saddest moment of his life.

A few months later, astronauts Gordon Cooper and Charles (Pete) Conrad orbited Earth for eight days. They proved that people could stay in space long enough to go to the moon and back.

Then on Christmas Eve, 1968, astronauts Frank Borman, James Lovell, and William Anders orbited the moon ten times. They wished everyone on Earth a merry Christmas from space. They proved that people could travel all the way to the moon and return safely to Earth.

Finally, the Americans felt they were ready to put a person on the moon.

Steps to the Moon

1961–1967—Probes take pictures

1965—Space walk

1965—Eight days in space

1968—Moon orbit

To the Moon!

On July 16, 1969, a rocket blasted off from Cape Kennedy, Florida. The rocket carried a spacecraft called *Apollo 11*.

The *Apollo 11* spacecraft had two parts. Each part was called a *module*.

The first module was the *command and service module*, or CSM. The CSM would carry three astronauts through space and into orbit around the moon.

The second module was the *lunar module*, or LM. Once *Apollo 11* was in orbit, the LM would separate and carry two astronauts to the moon's surface. After they had walked on the moon, the LM would carry them back to the CSM. Then all three astronauts would return to Earth.

Command and
service module

Lunar module

There were dangers every step of the way. Anything that went wrong could ruin the whole mission. A tiny mistake could mean death for all three astronauts.

The astronauts called the lunar module the Eagle.

Moon Walk

On July 20, 1969, four days after the launch, *Apollo 11* went into orbit around the moon. A few hours later, the LM landed on the moon's surface.

When the LM landed on the moon, they sent a message to Earth that said: "The Eagle has landed."

At 9:56 P.M. Eastern Standard Time, American astronaut Neil Armstrong became the first person to set foot on the moon. Fellow astronaut Edwin "Buzz" Aldrin followed a few minutes later.

Neil Armstrong had thought very carefully about what his first words from the moon should be. When he stepped onto the moon's surface, this is what he said:

"That's one small step for a man, one giant leap for mankind."

He meant that landing on the moon was an accomplishment the whole world could be proud of.

 The astronauts left a sign on the moon that read WE CAME IN PEACE FOR ALL MANKIND.

Neil Armstrong and Buzz Aldrin walked on the moon for about two hours. They planted an American flag. They sent messages telling the world how beautiful the moon was—and how beautiful Earth looked from space.

The following morning, Armstrong and Aldrin blasted off from the moon's surface and joined their fellow astronaut, Mike Collins, in the CSM. Then all three astronauts returned safely to Earth.

Their mission had gone perfectly.

People all over the world celebrated the safe return of the three American "moon men."

Moon Suits
and Moon Buggies

Astronauts used moon buggies on three moon missions. All three moon buggies are *still* on the moon!

Moon suits allowed the astronauts to walk on the moon's surface.

Moon buggy

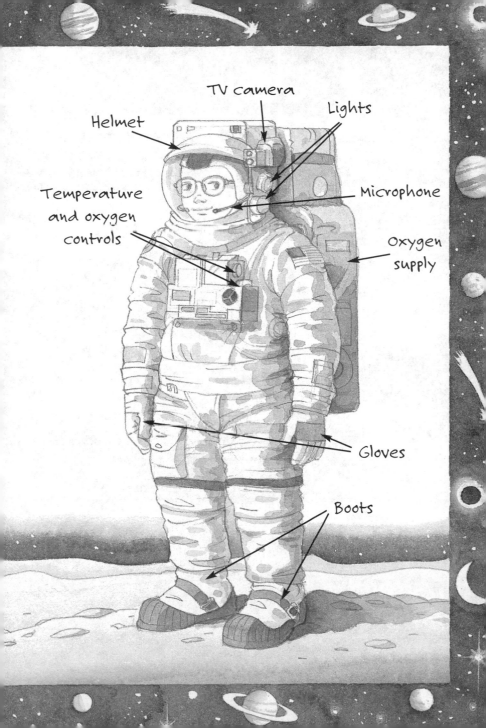

7

Space Travel Today

There were five more American moon landings between 1969 and 1972. During that time, the Soviets kept trying to put cosmonauts on the moon. They were never successful.

Finally, the Americans and the Soviets agreed to plan a mission together. In 1975, an American spacecraft joined with a Soviet spacecraft in orbit. The cosmonauts and astronauts shook hands. They shared a meal as they orbited Earth together.

The space race was over. A new era of space cooperation had begun.

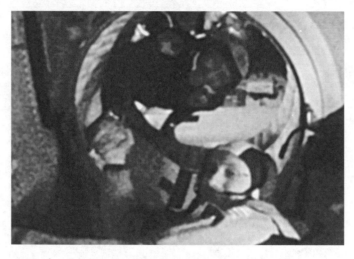

In July 1975, astronaut Thomas P. Stafford shook hands with cosmonaut Alexei A. Leonov in space.

Space Stations

When they weren't able to land a man on the moon, the Soviets began working on a different kind of space project. They began to build *space stations*.

A space station is like a house in space. There is room inside for space travelers to eat and sleep. There is also room for them to conduct many kinds of experiments.

An *experiment* is a test to find out or prove something.

Between 1971 and 1982, the Soviet Union launched seven space stations. All these space stations were named *Salyut* (sal-YOOT). *Salyut* is the Russian word for "salute." Soviet leaders named the space stations as a salute to Yuri Gagarin.

Space stations can stay in space for many years.

The United States has put only one space station into orbit. It was called *Skylab*. *Skylab* was damaged during its launch in 1973 and used for only a few months.

In 1986, the Soviet Union launched a new kind of space station. It was called *Mir* (MEER). *Mir* is the Russian word for "peace."

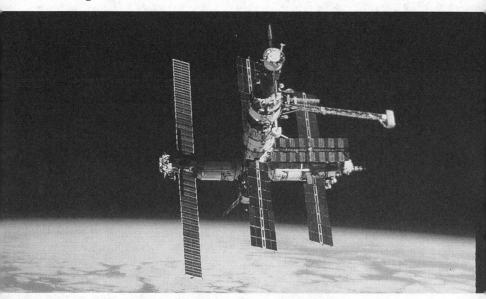

Mir was supposed to orbit Earth for five years. With new parts and many repairs, Mir stayed in space for 15 years.

Space travelers from many countries visited *Mir* while it was in orbit around Earth. Some stayed on board *Mir* for over a year. They proved that people could live in space long enough to travel to other planets.

Mir was finally abandoned in 2001. It fell safely to Earth.

The International Space Station

Now several countries around the world are working together on a new space station. It is called the *International Space Station*, or ISS.

The first parts of the ISS were launched by Russia and the U.S. in 1998.

Like *Mir*, the ISS will be put together in space. When it is finished, it will be twice as big as a football field. From Earth, it will look like the brightest star in the sky.

Space Stations

Salyuts—1971-1982

Skylab—1973-1974

Mir—1986-2001

ISS—1998-present

The first space shuttle was launched in 1981.

The Space Shuttle

For many years, the spacecraft that took people into space were built for one mission only. Today, a new kind of spacecraft carries people into space. It is called the space shuttle. The space shuttle is the only spacecraft ever built that can be used more than once.

The space shuttle takes off like a rocket. It orbits Earth for up to two weeks. Then it returns to Earth and lands like an airplane.

Space shuttle <u>Columbia</u>

Parachutes help the space shuttle
slow down after landing.

The space shuttle carries astronauts to and from space stations. It is used to launch satellites. Space shuttle crews sometimes pick up broken satellites in space, repair them, then send them back into orbit.

106

Space shuttle crews have also per-
formed thousands of experiments. These
experiments help scientists understand
more about living and working in space.

Turn the page to learn more about the
parts of the space shuttle.

The Space Shuttle

The space shuttle has three main parts. All but one of the parts can be used over and over.

Orbiter—carries crew into space and back to Earth.

Cargo bay—part of orbiter where equipment is stored; also where crew performs experiments.

Fuel tank—carries rocket fuel to get shuttle into space. When fuel is used up, tank falls back through atmosphere and burns up.

Solid rocket boosters—help shuttle get off ground. Once shuttle is headed for space, they fall back to Earth.

Shuttle astronaut Mae Jemison

8

Living and Working in Space

Conditions in space are very different from those on Earth. There is no air to breathe. The temperature can be freezing cold or boiling hot. Without the protection of Earth's atmosphere, the sun's rays are very dangerous.

Spacecraft like the shuttle and the ISS are built to make humans as comfortable as possible in space. They have their own sup-

The <u>hull</u> is
the outside
covering of a
ship, plane,
or spacecraft.

ply of air. They have temperature controls. They have hulls and windows that block the sun's dangerous rays.

Weightlessness

There's one difference between being in space and being on Earth that scientists can't control. It's called *weightlessness*.

Astronauts in orbit feel weightless because their spacecraft is constantly "falling" through space toward Earth. Luckily, the spacecraft is traveling so fast that Earth curves away from it as it falls, so it never hits the ground. But everything inside the spacecraft (including astronauts) floats around as if it had no weight at all.

Weightlessness affects everything astronauts do in space. There is no up or down. Tools, pencils, and notepads float around them as they work. They bathe with wet towels because water wouldn't stay in a tub!

Food trays have to be stuck to tables. Food has to be sticky so it will stay on a fork. Cookies are a little bit gooey so there won't be crumbs floating all over the place!

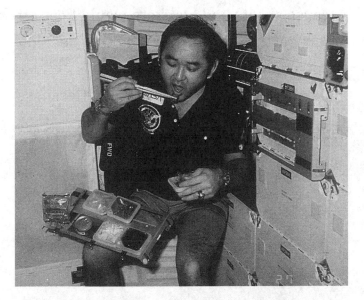

Ellison Onizuka was the first Japanese American astronaut. Sadly, he and six other astronauts were killed when the space shuttle Challenger exploded in 1986.

There's no
day or night
in space.

Space toilets have seatbelts and foot straps. They don't flush with water. Instead, they flush by sucking air like a vacuum cleaner.

When it's time to sleep, most astronauts strap themselves into sleeping bags attached to the walls. That's because sheets and blankets would float off a regular bed—and so would a sleeping astronaut!

On long space flights, weightlessness

can cause serious problems. Astronauts' muscles and bones can become very weak. So astronauts spend part of every day doing exercises. Otherwise, they might not be able to walk when they got back to Earth!

Even with all the problems, most astronauts say they enjoy traveling in space. Nearly all agree that weightlessness is *fun*!

When a spacecraft is orbiting Earth, the sun rises and sets about every 90 minutes!

The Jack Files:
Life in Outer Space

Is there life anywhere in the universe besides Earth?

No one knows. But many astronomers think the universe is so gigantic that it's unlikely Earth is the *only* place with living creatures.

The SETI Program

SETI stands for Search for Extraterrestrial Intelligence. *Extraterrestrial* means "from beyond Earth." Astronomers in the SETI program listen for radio messages from space creatures. They also send messages far into space. So far, they haven't gotten an answer!

SETI astronomers use the Arecibo radio
telescope in Puerto Rico to listen for
messages from space.

UFOs

UFOs are *unidentified flying objects*. Some people think space creatures visit Earth in UFOs. But there has never been any proof that UFOs exist.

UFOs are sometimes called *flying saucers*. That's because UFOs in stories and movies are often round and flat.

Space Aliens

Extraterrestrial creatures are also called *aliens*. Scientists can only imagine what aliens might look like. They make guesses based on the conditions of the planets aliens might live on.

What do *you* think space aliens might look like?

9

The Future

In ancient times, people built stone towers to study the sky more closely. Today, scientists are planning projects that could take people into space for a weekend vacation!

Giant spinning space stations might use artificial gravity to make visitors more comfortable in space. These kinds of space stations could even be used as hotels for tourists.

Space colonies might someday be built on the moon or Mars. These would be like towns with their own supplies of air and food. People could spend many years in a space colony without returning to Earth.

All these projects are very far in the future. The next big step in space travel will probably be landing on Mars. Many scientists believe this could happen in the next 20 years.

Who will be the first person to set foot on Mars? Sally Ride, the first American woman to travel in space, has an answer:

Sally Ride

"The first person to land on Mars is alive today. He or she is probably a kid involved in a science project somewhere in the world right now. And it's going to be a wonderful day when that kid plants the flag of Earth into the red soil of Mars."

Who knows? Maybe the kid Sally Ride is talking about is YOU!

Doing More Research

There's a lot more you can learn about space and space travel. The fun of research is seeing how many different sources you can explore.

Books

Most libraries and bookstores have lots of books about astronomy and the history and science of space travel.

Here are some things to remember when you're using books for research:

1. You don't have to read the whole book. Check the table of contents and the index to find the topics you're interested in.

2. Write down the name of the book.

When you take notes, make sure you write down the name of the book in your notebook so you can find it again.

3. Never copy exactly from a book.

When you learn something new from a book, put it in your own words.

4. Make sure the book is <u>nonfiction</u>.

Many books tell make-believe stories of space adventures and alien creatures. These books are called *science fiction* books. Science fiction books are fun to read, but not good for research. Research books have real facts and tell true stories. They are called *nonfiction*. A librarian or teacher can help you make sure the books you use for research are nonfiction.

Here are some good nonfiction books about space travel:

- *All About Space* by Ian Graham
- *Finding Out About Rockets and Spaceflight* by Lynn Myring (Usborne Explainers series)
- *Finding Out About Sun, Moon and Planets* by Lynn Myring and Sheila Snowden (Usborne Explainers series)
- *The Kingfisher Young People's Book of Space* by Martin Redfern
- *The Mystery of Mars* by Sally Ride & Tam O'Shaughnessy
- *Space* (a Reader's Digest Pathfinders book)

Science

Museums and Planetariums

Many science museums have exhibits about space and space travel. Some museums also have planetariums. A planetarium is a special theater that can make you feel just like you're outside under the stars!

When you go to one of these museums or planetariums:

1. Be sure to take your notebook!
Write down anything you see that catches your interest. Draw pictures, too!

2. Ask questions.
There are almost always people at a museum or planetarium who can help you find what you're looking for.

3. Check the calendar.

Many museums and planetariums have special events and activities just for kids!

Here are some museums and planetariums with space exhibits:

- Adler Planetarium & Astronomy Museum, Chicago, Illinois

- Carnegie Science Center Pittsburgh, Pennsylvania

- Griffith Observatory Los Angeles, California

- Hayden Planetarium Rose Center for Earth and Space New York, New York

- New York Hall of Science Queens, New York

- Smithsonian National Air and Space Museum, Washington, D.C.

Videos

There are some great nonfiction videos about space. There are also lots of science fiction movies about make-believe space aliens, life on other planets, and space travel in the future. As with books, make sure the videos you use for research are nonfiction!

Check your library or video store for some nonfiction space videos.

CD-ROMs

CD-ROMs often mix facts with fun activities.

Ask your teacher or librarian to help you find CD-ROMs about space and space travel.

The Internet

Many Internet Web sites have lots of facts about space and space travel. Some also have games and activities that can help make learning about space even more fun.

Ask your teacher or your parents to help you find more Web sites like these:

- www.astronomy.com/content/static/ AstroForKids
- www.childrensmuseum.org/cosmicquest
- www.faahomepage.org/main.html
- www.jsc.nasa.gov/pao/ students
- www.pbs.org/wgbh/ nova/worlds

Good luck!

Index

Aldrin, Edwin
    "Buzz," 93, 95
aliens, 119
Anders, William, 90
Apollo 11, 90–95
Armstrong, Neil,
    93–94, 95
asteroid belt, the, 49
asteroids, 46, 49, 68
astronauts, 81, 84,
    87, 88–89, 90, 92,
    93, 94, 95, 96–97,
    99, 106, 110,
    112–113, 114, 115
astronomers, 14–21,
    28, 31, 32, 40, 45,
    59, 72, 77, 116
astronomy, 14–23

Belka, 85
Big Bang, the, 27–30

billion, 29
booster rockets, 109
Borman, Frank, 90

calendars, 14
cargo bay, 109
Charon, 72
Collins, Mike, 95
comets, 46, 48, 50,
    59, 67, 68, 72
command and
    service module,
    the (CSM), 92, 94
Conrad, Charles, 89
Cooper, Gordon, 89
Copernicus, 15–17,
    19, 20
core (of the sun),
    the, 36
cosmonauts, 81, 84,
    99

days, 47

Eagle, 93
Earth (references
    throughout)
Explorer, 81

flying saucers, *see*
    unidentified
    flying objects
fuel tank, 108

Gagarin, Yuri,
    81–82, 83, 101
galaxies, 31
Galileo, 17–19, 20
gas giants, 64, 67
Glenn, John, 84
gravity, 20, 46, 48,
    61, 78, 112
Hubble Space
    Telescope, the,
    24

hull, 112

International Space
    Station, the
    (ISS), 103, 104,
    111

Jemison, Mae, 110
Jupiter, 18, 49,
    64–65

Kennedy, John F.,
    83, 87

landing module, the
    (LM), 92, 93
law of gravity, the,
    20; *see also*
    gravity
light-years, 32–33
Lippershey, Hans,
    22, 23
Lovell, James, 90

Luna, 60

Mars, 49, 62–63, 122,
123, 124
Mercury, 54–55
meteor showers, 51
meteorites, 52–53
meteoroids, 46,
51–53
meteors, 51–52
Milky Way, the, 31
million, 28
Mir, 102–103, 104
moon, Earth's, 18,
20, 25, 42, 49,
54, 60–61, 72,
122
landings on, 83,
87–97, 99
moon buggies, 96–97
moon suits, *see*
space suits
moon walk, 93–95

moons, 18, 46, 48,
63, 65, 66, 72, 80

Neptune, 70–71
Newton, Sir Isaac,
20, 23
nuclear reactions, 36

Onizuka, Ellison,
113
orbiter, 108
orbits, 46–47, 81, 84,
85, 89, 90
outer space:
definition of, 77
life in, 116–119
living in, 111, 115

planets, 14, 15, 16,
24, 27, 46, 47, 48,
49, 54–75
remembering
names of, 74–75

Pluto, 72
probes, 88
prominences, 39
Proxima Centauri,
    32
Ptolemy, 15, 16

red giant, 40
Ride, Sally, 124–125
rings, 67, 68, 71
rockets, 78–79, 80,
    90–91, 104
rotation, 47

Salyut, 101, 104
satellites, 80, 81,
    106
Saturn, 18, 66–67
Search for
    Extraterrestrial
    Intelligence, the
    (SETI), 116

Shepard, Alan, 84
Skylab, 102, 104
Sol, 42
solar eclipses, 42–43
solar flares, 38
solar system, the,
    45–75
    creation of, 45–46
    parts of, 46–53
    planets in, 54–75
space colonies, 122
space race, the,
    80–100
space shuttle, the,
    104–109, 111
space stations,
    100–101, 106, 121
space suits, 88,
    96–97
space travel, 77–85
space walk, 88–89,
    90

spacecraft, 78–79, 80, 82, 88, 89, 91, 92, 99, 104, 111–112, 114; *see also names of specific space- craft*
Sputnik, 80
stars, 14, 15, 18, 21, 24, 27, 30, 31, 32–33, 35, 41, 45
Strelka, 85
sun, the, 15, 16, 20, 21, 27, 31, 32, 35–43, 45, 46, 47, 48, 49, 50
sunspots, 37–38

telescopes, 17–18, 22–25
Tereshkova, Valentina, 85

trillion, 29

unidentified flying objects (UFOs), 118
universe, the, 21, 27–31, 41, 116
Uranus, 68–69

Venus, 18, 56–57
Very Large Telescope, the, 25

weightlessness, 112–115
White, Ed, 88–89
white dwarf, 40

years, 47
yellow dwarf, 40

Titanic

A NONFICTION
COMPANION TO
Tonight
on the
Titanic

Will Usborne
and Mary Pope Osborne

If you liked *Tonight on the Titanic,*
you'll love finding out the facts
behind the fiction in

Magic Tree House®
Research Guide
TITANIC

A nonfiction companion to
Tonight on the Titanic

It's Jack and Annie's very own guide
to the mysteries of the *Titanic!*

Magic Tree House® Books

#1: Dinosaurs Before Dark

#2: The Knight at Dawn

#3: Mummies in the Morning

#4: Pirates Past Noon

#5: Night of the Ninjas

#6: Afternoon on the Amazon

#7: Sunset of the Sabertooth

#8: Midnight on the Moon

#9: Dolphins at Daybreak

#10: Ghost Town at Sundown

#11: Lions at Lunchtime

#12: Polar Bears Past Bedtime

#13: Vacation Under the Volcano

#14: Day of the Dragon King

#15: Viking Ships at Sunrise

#16: Hour of the Olympics

#17: Tonight on the *Titanic*

#18: Buffalo Before Breakfast

#19: Tigers at Twilight

#20: Dingoes at Dinnertime

#21: Civil War on Sunday

#22: Revolutionary War on Wednesday

#23: Twister on Tuesday

#24: Earthquake in the Early Morning

#25: Stage Fright on a Summer Night

**Other books by Mary Pope Osborne
and Will Osborne:**

Picture books:
Kate and the Beanstalk by Mary Pope Osborne
Mo and His Friends by Mary Pope Osborne
Moonhorse by Mary Pope Osborne
Rocking Horse Christmas by Mary Pope Osborne

First chapter books:
The *Magic Tree House®* series by Mary Pope Osborne

For middle-grade readers:
Adaline Falling Star by Mary Pope Osborne
American Tall Tales by Mary Pope Osborne
The Deadly Power of Medusa by Mary Pope Osborne
    and Will Osborne
Favorite Greek Myths by Mary Pope Osborne
Favorite Medieval Tales by Mary Pope Osborne
Favorite Norse Myths by Mary Pope Osborne
Jason and the Argonauts by Mary Pope Osborne
    and Will Osborne
Joe Magarac by Will Osborne
The Life of Jesus in Masterpieces of Art
    by Mary Pope Osborne

Mermaid Tales from Around the World
    by Mary Pope Osborne
My Brother's Keeper by Mary Pope Osborne
My Secret War by Mary Pope Osborne
One World, Many Religions by Mary Pope Osborne
Spider Kane and the Mystery Under the May-Apple
    (#1) by Mary Pope Osborne
Spider Kane and the Mystery at Jumbo Nightcrawler's
    (#2) by Mary Pope Osborne
Standing in the Light by Mary Pope Osborne
13 Ghosts: Strange but True Stories by Will Osborne

For young-adult readers:

Haunted Waters by Mary Pope Osborne

MARY POPE OSBORNE and WILL OSBORNE have been married for a number of years and live in New York City with their Norfolk terrier, Bailey. Mary is the author of over fifty books for children, and Will has worked for many years in the theater as an actor, director, and playwright. Together they have co-authored two books of Greek mythology and the Magic Tree House Research Guides.

"One of the highlights of our research for *Space* was visiting the New York Hall of Science, which is run by our friend Dr. Alan J. Friedman. While we were there, we saw models of all the planets and two real space rockets! We also explored a different kind of space—cyberspace! We spent a lot of time on the Internet, finding out the most recent facts about telescopes, space stations, and space shuttle missions. And sometimes, we just looked up at the stars and thought about the universe and our little corner of it here on Earth."